Two African Countries

Elizabeth Paren and Gill Stacey

OXFORD

UNIVERSITY PRESS

OXFORD
UNIVERSITY PRESS

Great Clarendon Street, Oxford OX2 6DP

Oxford University Press is a department of the University of Oxford.
It furthers the University's objective of excellence in research, scholarship,
and education by publishing worldwide in

Oxford New York
Auckland Bangkok Buenos Aires Cape Town Chennai
Dar es Salaam Delhi Hong Kong Istanbul Karachi Kolkata
Kuala Lumpur Madrid Melbourne Mexico City Mumbai
Nairobi São Paulo Shanghai Taipei Tokyo Toronto

Oxford is a registered trade mark of Oxford University Press
in the Uk and in certain other countries

Published in the United Kingdom
by Oxford University Press

Text © Elizabeth Paren and Gill Stacey 2001

Database right Oxford University Press (maker)

First published 2001
10 9 8 7 6 5 4 3 2

British Library Cataloguing in Publication Data

Data available

ISBN 0 19 917389 3
Available in packs
People of Different Lands Pack of Four (one of each book) ISBN 0 19 917390 7
People of Different Lands Class Pack (six of each book) ISBN 0 19 917391 5

Printed in Hong Kong

Acknowledgements

The Publisher would like to thank the following for permission
to reproduce photographs:

Ashanti Gold: p. 23 (top); Botswanacraft: p. 26 (both); Corel: pp 6 left), 25 (top), (middle), 27 (bottom right);
De Beers: p. 19 (left); Hutchison Library/Michael Macintyre: p. 16 (right); Hutchison Library/M Kahn: p. 22 (top);
Hutchison Library/Mary Jelliffe: p. 22 (middle); Hutchison Library/Crispin Hughes: p. 30; Hutchison Library/Liba Taylor:
p. 23 (bottom); Illustrative options: p. 9 (bottom); Images of Africa Photobank/David Keith Jones: p. 7 (left); Images
of Africa/Vanessa Burger: p. 7 (bottom right), 27; Images of Africa Photobank/Carla Signorini Jones: p. 9 (top); Panos
Pictures/Trygve Bolstad: p. 10 (left); Panos Pictures/Liba Taylor: p. 11 (middle); Panos Pictures/David Reed: pp 14 (top),
17 (bottom), 22 (bottom); Panos Pictures/Caroline Penn: p. 17 (top); Panos Pictures/Betty Press: p. 20 (left); Panos
Pictures/Bruce Paton: p. 21 (left); Panos Pictures/Steve Thomas: p. 29 (top); Robert Estall Photo Library/Carol
Beckwith/Angela Fisher: pp 24 (top), (bottom), 25 (bottom,); Petra Röhr-Rouéndaal: pp 5 (left), 11 (left), 12, 21
(top); Still Pictures/Ron Giling: p. 4 (top right); Still Pictures/E Duigenan – Christian Aid: p. 4 (bottom left); Still
Pictures/Jorgen Schytte: pp 6 (right), 10 (right), 13 (top right), 15 (top), 16 (left), 20 (right), 28 (bottom); Still
Pictures/Jonas Ekstromer: p. 18 (left); Still Pictures/ Chris Caldicott: p. 28 (top); Tropix/M Auckland: pp 5 (right), 15
(bottom), 29 (bottom); Tropix/M-V Birley: p. 8; Tropix/J Woollard: pp 13 (middle), 19 (right); Tropix/Brydon: p. 14
(bottom); Tropix/G Roberts: p. 18 (bottom).

Front cover: Petra Röhr-Rouéndaal (top right); Botswanacraft (bottom left); Corel (background)
Back cover: Robert Estall Photo Library/Carol Beckwith/Angela Fisher

Illustrations are by Petra Röhr-Rouéndaal.
Maps on pp 6–8 are by Richard Morris
Globes by Geo Atlas

Contents

Welcome to Botswana and Ghana

There are 47 countries in Africa. In this book we will look at two of them, Botswana and Ghana.

Botswana and Ghana have a lot in common. For example, they are both young countries, with a high proportion of the population under the age of 18.

This book looks at other similarities between the two countries – and at many differences too.

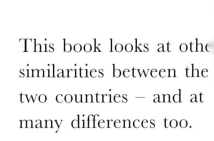

FACT BOX		Botswana	Ghana
	Population	about 1.5 million	about 18 million
	Capital	Gaborone	Accra
	Main peoples	Setswana, Kalanga	Akan, Ewe, Mole-Dagomba

flag of Botswana

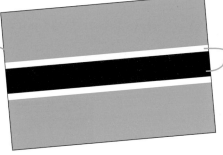

lue for water:
ater is very
recious to the
eople of Botswana.

White and black for
the people: these
colours show how the
people live peacefully
together.

flag of Ghana

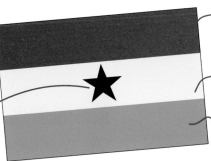

Red for the blood of
freedom fighters

Gold for the minerals

The black star for
African freedom

Green for the land

s book is about the everyday lives of
ple in these two African countries. It tells
what the children learn at school, what
do when they go home, and where they
hopping. It might also make you want to
Ghana and Botswana one day!

What is the land like?

Ghana is a country in West Africa. It lies in the **tropics**, just north of the Equator in the Tropic of Cancer.

Most of the land in Ghana is flat and less than 150 metres above sea level.

The coast of Ghana is over 500 kilometres long. Behind it are salt water **lagoons** and low-lying **plains**.

Tropic of Cancer

▲ Lake Volta, in the centre of Ghana, is the world's largest man-made lake. It is 400 kilometres long. The dams at Akosombo and Kpong provide most of Ghana's electricity.

▲ About one-third of Ghana is rainfore. In the north, there are fewer trees a more grassland.

Key
● savannah grassland
● rainforest
● coastal plains

Black Volta
White Volta
Oti
Tano
GHANA
Lake Volta
Akosombo Dam
Accra
Atlantic Ocean
0   100

6

thousand kilometres away from
na is Botswana. It lies south of the
tor and the Tropic of Capricorn
es the country. Botswana has no
line.

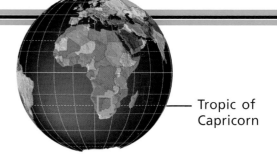

—— Tropic of
Capricorn

Most of Botswana is about
1100 metres above sea level
and forms a basin. This basin
is part of the Kalahari, which
is mostly semi-desert with dry
grassland and short trees.

In the south-west the land is
desert, where little grows.

rth-west Botswana, the Okavango river
ds out in a wide **delta**. The water
into the sand, leaving a huge **swamp**.

A game reserve in the central
Kalahari

▼

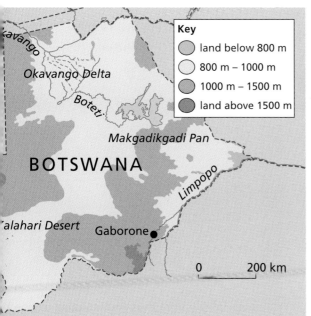

Key
- land below 800 m
- 800 m – 1000 m
- 1000 m – 1500 m
- land above 1500 m

Okavango

Okavango Delta

Boteti

Makgadikgadi Pan

BOTSWANA

Limpopo

Kalahari Desert   Gaborone ●

0   200 km

What is the weather like?

Both Ghana and Botswana lie in the tropics. However, their climates are very different.

Ghana has a tropical climate. There are two main seasons: the dry season and the rainy season. It is hot almost all year round. In the day, the temperature often reaches 30° C.

The dry season lasts from November to March. The weather is hot and dry in the north. In the south it is hot and sticky.

In the dry season, th **harmattan** wind blo from the Sahara De It brings cooler nigh and covers everythin with fine dust and s

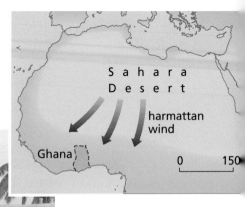

Sahara Desert

harmattan wind

Ghana

0   150

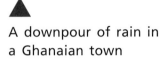

A downpour of rain in a Ghanaian town

The rainy season lasts from April to October. There are thunderstorms and very heavy rainfall. In between the storms, the days are hot and sunny.

These graphs show the rainfall in the tw capital cities.

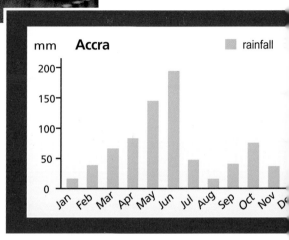

mm **Accra**   rainfall

200
150
100
50
0

Jan Feb Mar Apr May Jun Jul Aug Sep Oct Nov D

seasons in Botswana are more like those in Europe, a definite difference between summer and winter.

Summer lasts from November to April. This is when it rains, with thunderstorms in the late afternoon. Often there is not enough rain, and the farmers worry about their crops.

...ner days in Botswana ...ot, with temperatures ...times reaching 30°C.

Batswana dress up warmly for the winter days. ▶

Winter lasts from May to October. Then the days can be warm but dry and the nights can be cold. There are sometimes frosts.

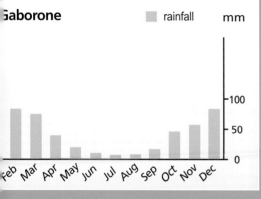

Gaborone   ▪ rainfall   mm

Going to primary school

In both countries, most children walk to school.
Some of them have to walk several miles.

 A primary classroom in Botsw

An outside classroom in Ghana

Some primary schools have bright
classrooms with chairs, tables, and
plenty of materials. However,
many schools have basic furniture
and few materials.

FACT BOX		
Ghana	**Botswana**	
School starts at 8.30am and finishes at 3.30pm.	School starts at 7am and finishes at 12.30pm.	
Children learn in their own language.	Children learn in their own language un Year 3. Then they learn in English.	
Most children learn Maths, Science, Religion, English, History, and Life Skills.	Children learn Setswana, Maths, Englisl Science, and Social Studies.	
Children have to wear school uniform. Most children wear the same colours – yellow and brown.	Most children wear school uniform.	

Ye fre me Kwabena. Ye frewo sen?

...abena is from Ghana.
...s saying:
...ame is Kwabena. What's your name?
...bena's own language is Twi.

Leina lame ke Neo. Leina la gago ke mang?

Neo is from Botswana.
She is saying:
My name is Neo. What's your name?
Neo's own language is Setswana.

...ak time

...reak time all children like to have a
...k. They may bring their own food, or
...may buy from women who sell food
...de the school.

...oth countries, children like to eat fruit.
...hana, fried **plantain**, roasted **maize**,
...uts, and doughballs are popular snacks.
...e **Batswana** children bring crisps and
...lwiches to eat. Many have bread and tea.

▲
This Ghanaian woman is
cooking and selling doughballs.

At break time, children play
games. Boys prefer football.
Girls often play skipping or
jumping games.

◀ These Batswana children
are playing a dancing
game in the playground.

11

After school

All children have chores to do when they return from school. This girl, like many others, does chores around the home.

Walking home from school

Looking after little brother

Drinking tea

Cleaning

Fetching water from the well

Helping to prepare food

Doing homework

Playing

Children may help to earn money for the family.

◀ These Ghanaian girls are selling tomatoes in the market.

have to do their
ework too. In Ghana
might then help with
ishing or work on the
a farm. Some boys look
cattle.

in Botswana have to
after cattle or goats.
y might collect firewood
donkey cart.

This Ghanaian boy is helping
fishermen with their nets.
His payment will be a bucket
of fish.

These Batswana boys are
taking a break from their
herding.

Some children, mostly in the towns, are lucky
enough to have televisions or computers.

Children in towns still have to do some
chores. They might go to the shops, look after
younger brothers or sisters, prepare food, or
help in the garden.

They play the same kind of games as children
in the **rural** areas. Football is always popular.

Farming and food

In both countries many people live in **rural** areas. Every family farms some land. Some men and women are full-time farmers; some have other jobs as well.

Most farmers grow food for their own families. Families usually only have a small plot of land, and do most of the work by hand. Most families keep animals, such as chickens or goats.

A Batswana woman weeds the maize crop – women do most of the daily work on the farm. ▶

Here are just some of the food crops they grow in Ghana.

YAM
MANGO
MAIZE
OKRA
ONIONS
PLANTAIN
GHANA

Ghanaians like spicy food. They eat a **starch** dish with meat or vegetable stew. The most popular starch dish is fufu, made from yams or cassava.

In Ghana, many small farmers also grow some crops to sell. The most important crop is cocoa.

Women work hard to pound the ▶ fufu until it is completely smooth.

These Ghanaian women are threshing. People in both countries always help each other when there is extra work to be done on the farm, such as clearing the land, or bringing in the harvest.

...e are just some of the food crops ... grow in Botswana.

...e Batswana like to eat mopane ...ms. These are the **larvae** of the ...pane moth. People collect the ...ms from mopane trees, then dry ... worms and ... them.

MELON

MILLET

BEANS

SPINACH

MAIZE

BOTSWANA

... dried ...pane worms ... first steamed, ... then fried. ...ey are full of ...tein and ...erals.

Many Batswana families own some cows. They provide beef to sell, and also show how wealthy a family is.

15

Family life in rural areas

Many members of a family often live together. There may be grandparents, married sons and their wives, and all their children. This is called an "extended family".

In rural areas in Ghana each extended family lives in a compound. The compound is made up of several buildings for different members of the family.

Family compounds in a village near Accra. ▶

◀ Ghanaian women do all the cooking. They may have an indoor kitchen or an outdoc cooking area.

Women and men have their own separate areas for sleeping, cooking, and eating. Young children eat and sleep with their mothers.

ildren in both countries are seen as a
essing to the family.
1 the adults help to bring up the
ildren.
1ildren are expected always to show
spect to their elders.
1ildren may go to live with other
1atives for a few years.

otswana, many people have always lived
ery large villages. The chief and his family
in the middle of the village. There is a
ial enclosure for the chief's cattle. The rest
ne village is divided into wards. Groups of
ed families live in each ward. Each one
its own cattle enclosure.

ay, these large
ges also have
l roads, shops,
ols, and offices.

Batswana villages are
spread over a very
wide area. Some
villages have as many
as 40,000 people.

Living in the towns and cities

In both Ghana and Botswana, more and more people are living in the towns. Some people are well-off and live in big houses. For most people, life is harder. They have to live in poorer, crowded areas.

What is daily life like in the capital cities, Accra and Gaborone?

Most people g
work by bus,
or shared tax

The streets of Accra are always crowded
Street vendors are everywhere, selling
newspapers, roasted nuts, sweets – even
lottery tickets.

Accra is a lively, modern city with
many business and government offices,
shops, busy markets, museums, and
apartment blocks.

...ay work in shops, or

Some people have their own small businesses.

People like to eat out. Fast food is also very popular.

There are lots of places to go after work.

...tching sport, especially ...ball, is a popular ...kend activity in ...swana. Large crowds ...the Gaborone sports ...dium to watch a ...iety of events.

Many people work as diamond sorters in Gaborone. Diamonds from Botswana are used to make jewellery all over the world.

All kinds of shopping

Markets are the most popular place for shopping in Ghana. Ghanaians go to market both to buy and to sell. Markets are also the place to meet friends and catch up on the latest gossip.

In the larger markets you can buy almost anything. Many of the most successful traders in Ghana are women. ▶

▲

Department stores and supermarkets are popular places to shop in the towns, although prices are usually higher than in the markets.

People can also buy thing from roadside stalls. Trad and farmers sell food cro such as pineapples, mang and yams. People travellin out from the towns find their prices much lower.

Market prices are not fixed. Traders and customers always bargain before a price is ag

This hat would really suit you, Madam. Only 20 dollars.

What! I can buy 10 hats for that!

OK give 15 doll

atswana towns, people do
shopping in small shops,
rmarkets, or in shopping
s.

e traders sell goods by the
of the road. Some sell cheap
hes, or grass brooms, but
y sell fruit and vegetables.
re are carpenters, too, who
make furniture to order.

The Mall in Gaborone is where everyone likes to meet and shop.

Batswana who live in rural areas can buy everyday items at the village store. Many people drive into town once a month to buy all the other things they need.

Village stores sell things such as salt, sugar, soap, matches, clothes, pots, and pans.

A changing world

New road systems, fast-growing towns, and modern technology are changing Botswana and Ghana. Many people are leaving the rural areas to work in factories, offices, and mines.

Botswana was once very poor. Today, it is one of the richest countries in Africa. Its wealth comes from diamonds and other minerals in the desert.

Gaborone is one of the f growing cities in the wor

Changing lives: the San people of the desert

The San once moved around the desert finding everything they needed. They collected underground water and stored it in ostrich egg shells. They gathered fruits and seeds, and hunted wild animals. They liked to tell stories around the fire.

This San woman is making ostrich egg shell beads.

Today, mines, cattle farms, and game reserves are spreading into the desert. The San have had to find homes and work elsewhere.

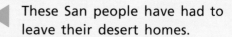
These San people have had to leave their desert homes.

...a is not a rich ...try, but its people ...working hard to ...ove their lives. ... hope that the ...ort of gold will ...them do this.

Modern machinery is used to process Ghanaian gold.

...anging lives: women in Ghana

...any men now leave their village homes to work in the ...wns. Women often have to bring up children and look ...ter the farms on their own.

...the past, Ghanaians believed that education was more ...portant for boys than girls. Today, many more girls go ...school and find good jobs.

...mall co-operatives ...elp women learn ...ew skills and earn ...oney for their ...milies. These ...hanaian women ...ork in a sewing ...o-operative.

Ghana – land of gold

The power of gold

There has always been gold in Ghana. Over 300 years ago, there was a forest kingdom called Ashanti. Its wealth and power came from gold.

The most important **symbol**, even today, of the power of the Ashanti people is the Golden Stool. This stool is solid gold. It is so precious that it is hidden away and is only seen on very special occasions.

The Golden Stool has pride of place next to the Ashanti king at this celebration. ▶

Kente cloth

The most famous craft in Ghana is weaving Kente cloth. Kente comes in many different colours and patterns. Each design is given a special name.

Once, only kings and queens could wear Kente. Today, it is the national costume for all Ghanaians, but is worn only for special occasions.

A Ghanaian festival: this girl is wearing Kente cloth and gold jewellery. ▶

:ivals

e are festivals throughout
a every month of the year.
yone enjoys festivals. They
a chance to dress up, to follow
urful processions, to listen to
tional music, and to dance.

y festival has a special
ning. Festivals remind people
nportant events in the past.
le show respect to their
tional leaders, and give
ks to God.

Festivals are often celebrated
with music and dance. ▶

Only men are allowed to weave Kente,
and the craft has always been passed
from father to son. Gilbert "Bobbo"
Ahiagble is a Master Weaver. When he
was three his father began to teach him
about weaving.

In 1999 Bobbo opened a school where
he teaches students to weave traditional
Kente.

Baskets and story-telling in Botswana

Making baskets

For hundreds of years, people in the north of Botswana have made baskets. They use them for storing food.

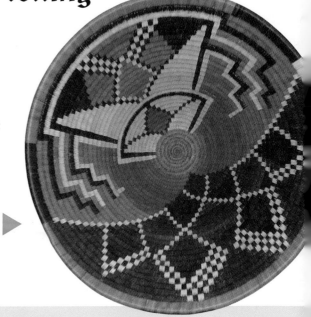

Today, many baskets are for sale. Their beautiful designs sell all over the world.

Mahurero Twapika

Mahurero lives with her family near the Okavango Delta. She is one of over two thousand women who make baskets. Mahurero's baskets have won prizes. Sometimes she visits Gaborone and teaches children how to make baskets.

Making baskets is hard work. Mahurero has to walk or ride on a donkey for half a day to find the palm shoots she needs. She cuts the shoots into strips and boils them with natural dyes. Then she can start weaving. It takes her a month to weave one basket.

ng stories

vana people love to tell stories.
story is told by the San people.

San people believe that a person's spirit can live in an animal's body.

Long ago, all the people and animals lived peacefully under the earth with Kaang, the Lord of all Life. They always had light.

Kaang created a world above the earth. First, he made an enormous tree. Then he dug a hole. He led the people and the animals through the hole up to the foot of the tree. Kaang told the people not to build any fires.

When it got dark the people were cold and frightened. They lit a fire. But the fire frightened the animals away. The people and animals would not live together any more.

Holidays with a difference

It is only recently that tourists have discovered the attractions of Ghana and Botswana.

Ghana – land of smiles

Enjoy Ghana's coast
Laze on the beautiful palm fringed beaches. Windsurf the Atlantic Ocean. Explore the unspoilt fishing village

Discover Ghana's rich p
Visit the ancient coastal and castles. Travel inland Kumasi – heart of the gr Ashanti Kingdom. Head north to the ancient mos of Larabanga.

Explore Ghana's natural beauty
See the rainforest from up high – along the treetop canopy walkway of Kakum National Park. See elephants and lions in Mole National Park. Take a boat on Lake Volta.

Bask in the warmth of Ghana
Bargain for crafts in the colourful markets. Share the excitement of our festivals.

Our country is the friendliest in West Africa!

isit Botswana – for the oliday of a lifetime!

sit the Okavango Delta

ep into your mekoro – the canoe at will take you through a tranquil rld of lilies and grasses. Watch e hippos, see the fish, hear the unting cry of the fish eagle. Watch unset you will never forget.

it Chobe National Park

dawn, see Chobe's mighty hants come out of the forest to k. Watch thousands of zebra rate across the wide, open plains.

t the Tsodilo Hills

amazing rock paintings in these remote hills. out how people and animals were living sands of years ago.

Visit the craft markets

Choose a beautifully-made souvenir of Botswana to take home. Will it be a basket, some jewellery, or a wall-hanging? It will be hard to choose.

29

Conclusion

Everyday life in Ghana and Botswana has many similarities.

- Most children live in rural areas and go to primary schools.
- Many are brought up in extended families.
- Most children have to do household chores before they play.
- People grow the food they eat and buy what cannot be grown in the market.
- Life in the towns is similar too, with people doing all kinds of work. Here there are shops, offices, supermarkets, sports stadiums, cinemas, and, usually, too many cars.
- Modern technology is beginning to change people's lives, especially in the towns. Office workers often use computers. Some people use the internet. Mobile phones are popular everywhere.

There are many differences as well.

The people in the two countries speak different languages and like different food. Their customs, the way they celebrate special occasions, and their music and dancing, are different too.

Glossary

Batswana The people of Botswana (can be used as a noun and as an adjective).

delta Low-lying land where a river divides up into many small branches.

export To sell things to another country.

harmattan A dry wind which carries sand and dust. It blows south from the Sahara Desert, usually during December and January.

lagoon A lake of sea water.

larvae The young of an insect, after they emerge from the egg and before they develop wings.

maize A type of cereal, also known as corn-on-the-cob. Maize can be cooked, used to make flour or oil, or to feed cattle.

plain A large area of flat land.

plantain Yellow or green fruit a tropical plant. Plantain look a large banana, but is cooked vegetable.

rural To do with the countrysi where most people live in villa and farm the land.

starch Food which may be eate the main part of a meal, such potatoes, rice, or yams.

swamp An area of low land wl is full of water.

symbol Something which repre a person or an idea. For exam the Golden Stool is the symbo the Ashanti people.

tropics The area of the Earth's surface which lies between the Tropics of Capricorn and Can These are imaginary lines of latitude drawn around the Ear

vendor A person who sells sma things on the street.

Index